VR ON THE JOB
Understanding Virtual
and Augmented Reality

USING VR IN GAMING

Cathleen Small

Cavendish
Square

New York

Published in 2020 by Cavendish Square Publishing, LLC
243 5th Avenue, Suite 136, New York, NY 10016

Library of Congress Cataloging-in-Publication Data

Names: Small, Cathleen.
Title: VR in gaming / Cathleen Small.
Description: New York : Cavendish Square Publishing, 2020. | Series: VR on the job:
understanding virtual and augmented reality | Includes glossary and index.
Identifiers: ISBN 9781502645661 (pbk.) | ISBN 9781502645678
(library bound) | ISBN 9781502645685 (ebook)
Subjects: LCSH: Computer games--Design--Vocational guidance--Juvenile literature. |
Computer games--Programming--Vocational guidance--Juvenile literature. | Virtual reality
in electronic games--Juvenile literature. | Augmented reality--Juvenile literature.
Classification: LCC QA76.76.C672 S627 2020 | DDC 794.81--dc23

Editorial Director: David McNamara
Editor: Chet'la Sebree
Copy Editor: Nathan Heidelberger
Associate Art Director: Alan Sliwinski
Designer: Christina Shults
Production Coordinator: Karol Szymczuk
Photo Research: J8 Media

CONTENTS

1 OVERVIEW OF VR AND AR

For gamers, virtual reality provides the ultimate experience. It allows them to immerse themselves in the world of the game. Gaming can also be a social endeavor. Gamers form friendships with fellow gamers. Often those friendships exist solely in the game world, but sometimes they become real-world friendships too. Regardless of why a gamer plays, virtual reality (VR) provides an experience unmatched by any other gaming experience. VR's counterpart, augmented reality (AR), provides a similar but slightly different experience that still allows the gamer a more immersive experience than a traditional game.

Opposite: VR headsets take players' gaming experiences to the next level!

VR AND AR: RELATED TECHNOLOGIES

At first glance, VR and AR might seem the same. It's true that they both alter reality in the context of the gaming world, and they both provide a more immersive experience for players. However, the two technologies differ after that point.

The two technologies' names accurately describe how they differ. In the computing world, the word "virtual"

With VR, players are completely immersed in the world of the game.

means something that doesn't physically exist but seems to exists through software and hardware. Software is the computer program responsible for this digital landscape. Hardware is the actual equipment, such as a headset, that allows the user to experience what has been programmed into the software. Through the software programs and hardware devices, the VR world completely replaces the real world for the player.

For gamers, the virtual world feels very real. They are, of course, aware that it's not real. However, the experience is so realistic and so immersive that players feel as if they are part of the game world. Virtual reality always involves hardware to immerse the player in the environment. Usually, this hardware comes in the form of a special VR headset and sometimes a VR hand controller. This hardware can also include bodysuits that help users experience sensations from the virtual worlds more fully.

In contrast, the word "augment" means to make something better by adding to it. In augmented reality, the user sees the real world. However, it is augmented by additions made to it by software. A good example of this type of reality is the game *Pokémon Go*. In the game, players explore real-world geography through their mobile devices' global positioning system (GPS). Pokémon characters are then overlaid on top of the real-world geography on the phone's screen so that they appeared to be present in real-world locations. Game players navigate their real world, trying through their phones to capture these Pokémon characters. In this way, game elements like the

Pokémon appear to exist in the real world through the magic of augmented reality.

characters have been added to the real-world scenery in the player's phone.

AR also involves hardware. However, sometimes a smartphone is all that's needed for an AR game. *Pokémon Go* requires only a smartphone, for example.

HISTORY OF VR

Both VR and AR are relatively new technologies in the grand scheme of computing history. However, it's interesting to look back at their histories and recent development.

One of the early milestones in virtual reality was when filmmaker Morton Heilig introduced his Sensorama. He patented it in 1962, meaning he was the only person legally allowed to develop the invention. The Sensorama was a booth that used smell, sound, vibrations, and other sensory elements to give people the impression that they were inside a virtual 3D world. However, he never fully developed it. While working on the Sensorama, Heilig also designed a head-mounted 3D television display. Head-mounted displays require that the device actually be attached to the user's head in order to track the user's movements.

Computer scientist Ivan Sutherland picked up where Heilig had left off. Sutherland created what many consider the first VR head-mounted display in 1968. His headset immersed the user in a world of wireframe shapes that changed in perspective as the user moved their head. Wireframe models are a type of 3D graphic. They are quite basic, usually just featuring the outlines of the 3D object or space. The reality created by Sutherland's device wasn't terribly realistic, given that our world doesn't exist in wireframe shapes. However, this headset did serve the purpose of immersing users in an interactive virtual world. Unfortunately, the technology never made it to the mainstream market. The headset was far too heavy for users to wear without it being mounted to the ceiling.

In 1982, Thomas Furness developed a flight simulator that he presented to the Air Force. Following this creation, he developed a VR headset flight simulator that later became known as the Super Cockpit. This invention led many to consider Furness the grandfather of virtual reality.

The Super Cockpit featured a 3D cockpit experience that a pilot could wear. It was used as a training tool for aspiring pilots. It allowed them to control a virtual plane using gestures, speech, and eye movements.

Despite these early VR inventions, it was a while before the technology moved into the gaming industry. In the early 1990s, gaming console manufacturer Sega created the first VR headset designed to be used in household gaming. However, the product never launched. Sega claimed they were concerned that the virtual effect was so realistic that users might hurt themselves

Morton Heilig's Sensorama is probably the earliest example of VR in action.

while wearing it. They also reported that some early users experienced headaches and motion sickness. Sega decided to release the headset for arcade use instead.

HISTORY OF AR

Ivan Sutherland, creator of the first head-mounted VR display, is also considered to be the forefather of AR, as some of his work fell in that category. Augmented reality truly started, however, in the 1990s.

In 1992, Louis Rosenberg created Virtual Fixtures, which is considered the first immersive AR system. Rosenberg was an artificial intelligence pioneer who was working at the US Air Force Armstrong Labs. Virtual Fixtures equipped users with upper-body gear that allowed them to control two physical robots to perform tasks. A headset with a unique magnifier component allowed the user to manipulate the robot arms to perform physical tasks. This magnifier component made the robot arms appear as though they were the user's own arms.

Although that was some of the first AR technology, some of the earliest and most common uses of AR were by Fox Broadcasting Company. In the mid-1990s, the station started to use AR to project graphic elements during real-time sporting events. For instance, in 1998, Sportsvision's 1st and Ten computer system used AR to mark the first-down line or the line of scrimmage on a live televised football game. This technology continues to be used in various forms for sporting events today.

JACQUELYN FORD MORIE: ARTIST TURNED TECH PIONEER

Technology is typically a male-dominated field, especially where gaming is concerned. Although more and more women are joining the field, a 2016 game developers survey put the share of women in game development at only about 22 percent. However, among those few women in the game development industry, there are several pioneers. One of them is Jacquelyn Ford Morie. She is the founder of All These Worlds, a company that uses VR to create solutions for a wide variety of needs.

Morie wasn't always in the tech field. In fact, she earned her bachelor's and master's degrees in fine art. However, after completing her master's degree in fine art, Morie decided to earn a master's degree in computer science as well. Afterwards, she went on to develop graphic design and animation programs at the Ringling College of Art and Design. VR was an emerging field at the time, and it piqued Morie's interest. So, she became a researcher at the Visual System Lab at the University of Central Florida, which began her career in VR.

She combined her VR and art skillset to co-create *Virtopia*. It debuted in 1992 at the Florida Film Festival. *Virtopia* featured Morie's groundbreaking work on emotionally evocative VR. With her co-creator, Mike Goslin, she created eight VR worlds designed to provoke different emotional reactions.

Morie went on to become the head of computer technical and artistic training for Walt Disney Feature Animation. She continued to work in the entertainment industry with a number of studios. Eventually, her contributions to VR helped form the Institute for Creative Technologies at the University of Southern California.

AR has been used in football broadcasts for more than two decades.

In 1999, NASA jumped into the AR field when they began to use an AR system in some spacecrafts to assist with navigation during test flights.

More recently, AR has been used as a tool in many industries. For example, Volkswagen uses AR technology in an app that allows service mechanics to view the vehicle's internal workings when diagnosing and fixing a problem. Surgeons can use AR similarly to view the internal organs and functions of the body when performing surgery. AR is even used in more entertainment-based capacities. Snapchat uses AR in games built into the app in addition to photo filters that augment users' faces. And, of course, AR came roaring into the public interest when *Pokémon Go* was released.

FROM PLAY TO CAREER

VR and AR technology is very exciting. The good news is it is not just for pleasure or play. For avid gamers and VR/AR enthusiasts, a career that integrates these interests is a very real possibility. The future is bright for jobs in VR and AR for gaming. For instance, an eighteen-year-old gaming and VR enthusiast designed Oculus Rift, a VR headset that has made him quite a lot of money.

2 VR AND AR IN GAMING

While both VR and AR alter the perception of reality by incorporating computer-generated elements, the technologies are not entirely similar. VR, for example, generally requires more specialized hardware than AR does. VR applications for gaming have been more widespread than AR applications. However, with the success of *Pokémon Go*, that may not be the case for long.

VR APPLICATIONS IN GAMING

There are hundreds of VR games on the market now. Many of the VR apps and games are similar to existing apps and games, but with the added

Opposite: Headsets are probably the most common piece of VR hardware, but VR gloves can help enhance the VR experience.

twist of full immersion. For example, Google Earth is an application that is accessible from any computer or smartphone. It provides people with 2D images of streets and neighborhoods at the touch of a finger or the click of a mouse. The Google Earth VR app takes it up a notch. Through this application, users can virtually walk through streets, climb mountains, fly over cities, and even explore space through a compatible headset. Although there are many different types of experiences, there is one thing that links all of these VR programs together. They all require some type of the hardware.

Oculus Technology

One of the best-known VR hardware manufacturers is Oculus VR, which makes the Oculus Rift, Oculus Go, and Oculus Quest headsets.

Oculus came into the public eye when a teenager named Palmer Luckey developed a prototype, or model, for a VR headset that would eventually become the Oculus Rift. The Rift headset is designed to be light and comfortable. This is an important feature in a VR headset. Oculus Touch motion controllers can be used with the Rift to provide hand control in the VR world. The Rift also features headphones so that gamers are immersed in the virtual world through sound as well. Finally, it comes with two sensors that help translate users' movements into virtual reality.

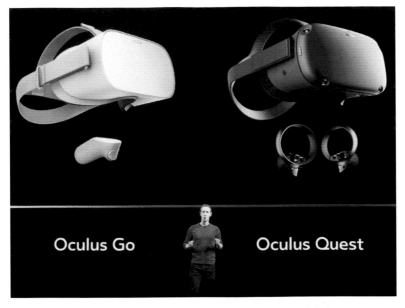

The Oculus technology was pioneered by a teenager named Palmer Luckey. The technology was then purchased by Facebook.

The Rift and its associated Touch controllers are compatible with hundreds of games and experiences. Games range from first-person shooters and driving games to casino games. Additionally, there are relaxation and meditation experiences, space discovery and other travel experiences, movies, and music that can be used with this VR headset.

In the gaming world, devices like the Oculus Rift allow games to be far more immersive than they typically are. Space-exploration games are nothing particularly new on traditional console or web-based games. However, using VR

The Gear VR headset was created by Oculus and Samsung to work with Samsung Galaxy smartphones.

technology, the gamer doesn't just control the movements of the player. The gamer becomes the player.

For example, the game *Lone Echo* for the Oculus Rift is extremely popular. It takes place in a space facility within the rings of the planet Saturn. Once players put on the Rift headset, they become Jack, who is basically a robot with extremely advanced artificial intelligence. As Jack, players move around the game environment with 360-degree gameplay, solving a space-themed mystery using interactive dialogue and futuristic tools.

The games and apps available for the Rift are far too many to mention, but they all share a common feature. They are incredibly realistic and immersive because of the refined technology provided by the Oculus Rift and Touch controllers. Additionally, the Rift is not the only VR technology offered by Oculus. They also have the Go and Quest, in addition to Oculus Gear. The latter is a portable VR headset used in combination with a mobile device. The Gear VR headset allows users to snap in their Samsung Galaxy smartphone to provide the VR experience. It comes with a hand controller for navigation and gameplay.

HTC

While Oculus VR is a major player in the VR hardware and software development realm, the company is far from the only one. Another major VR developer is HTC, which released the VIVE VR headset in 2016.

The VIVE headset is similar to the Oculus Rift in that it includes a headset, hand controllers, and base stations to track the user's play area. However, there are some subtle differences between them. The VIVE has sensors that track the users' external motion. In theory, the motion sensors mean that gamers can play in the entire room. The VIVE headset also incorporates a Chaperone feature that warns players about room boundaries. Additionally, a front-facing camera allows users to see glimpses of the real world so they can avoid real-world obstacles.

However, reviewers at *PC Magazine* in 2018 found that the whole-room VR experience offered by the VIVE was "tricky" to use and not quite as effortless as advertised. As of 2018, both the HTC VIVE and the Oculus Rift headsets still required the headsets to be connected to a Windows computer by wires. Reviewers found it difficult to access the full-room playability the VIVE headset offers without tripping over wires.

HTC has another VR headset option: the VIVE Pro. In addition to offering the features of the VIVE, the VIVE Pro offers superior image and audio quality for a more immersive experience. Perhaps most notably, the VIVE Pro offers a separate wireless adapter so users can avoid being tied to a computer. In 2018, however, it was far more expensive than the tethered VIVE headset.

The game offerings for both HTC headsets are similar to those offered for Oculus headsets. There are hundreds of available games VR users can download and play, offered at various prices.

Google

A mention of VR technologies would not be complete without mentioning Google's entry into the VR marketplace with its Daydream View and Cardboard devices.

Google's Cardboard is actually, as the name implies, made out of cardboard.

Like the Samsung Gear VR, the Daydream View is a headset in which users can place compatible Android smartphones and view the virtual world. Like other mobile VR headsets, the Daydream View comes with a motion-sensing hand controller to allow users to interact with the VR environment. The significant difference between the Daydream View and other mobile VR headsets is that the View is constructed of lightweight cloth material. This material makes it much lighter and more portable.

The Daydream View is actually Google's second VR headset. The company first entered the VR headset marketplace in 2014 with the Google Cardboard. It is

DANGERS OF VIRTUAL REALITY

As exciting as VR technology is, and as fun as the games and experiences are, it's worth noting that some researchers have suggested that there are some physical risks associated with continuous use of VR headsets. They've noted that these risks are particularly dangerous for children, whose brains are still developing.

Researchers at the University of Leeds in the United Kingdom found that the brain cannot process VR images in the same way that it processes images in real life. That's because in real life, eyes are looking at all 3D objects. The messages sent to the brain are based on the focus and eye direction needed to process 3D objects in a field of vision. In VR, however, the environment is technically all two-dimensional but appears to be three-dimensional. For this reason, our eyes focus differently. This has the same effect as visual surprise on the brain. The brain functions most efficiently when surprise is minimized. In the short term, this difference in vision and processing can cause headaches and sore eyes. It's unknown whether there are associated long-term effects.

Often, users of VR headsets have reported dizziness, disorientation, and nausea. Some of the users reporting these unpleasant side effects are also prone to motion sickness, so people who tend to get carsick may want to exercise caution. Finally, people who are prone to seizures should be very cautious about using VR. In fact, Oculus and other makers of VR equipment specifically warn against people with epilepsy using their equipment, as it can trigger seizures.

As with most things, moderation is key. Both Oculus and HTC recommend that users of their headsets take at least a ten-minute break every thirty minutes. Parents of children under the age of twelve are strongly encouraged to limit their children's VR time.

quite literally a cardboard viewer that users can place their Android or iOS smartphone in. Users can then run Cardboard-compatible applications on the smartphone. The Cardboard was intended to be very basic and give users a taste of VR. As such, it has no controllers, speakers, or headphones. It is simply a viewer.

AR APPLICATIONS IN GAMING

In some ways, AR in gaming is much simpler than VR. At its most basic, it can require only a smartphone. For example, *Pokémon Go* and similar AR games simply use a smartphone's GPS, camera, compass, clock, and accelerometer, which is a device that keeps track of the movements and orientation of the phone.

Pokémon Go uses an in-game map and then tracks a user's location by using the smartphone's built-in GPS technology. This technology works much in the same way Google Maps tracks a user's location to provide directions. The smartphone's camera places a Pokémon in view, using the smartphone's compass, accelerometer, and GPS to help gamers navigate right to the Pokémon. The smartphone's clock is used to place time-appropriate Pokémon in the user's environment. Nocturnal Pokémon, for example, appear when the smartphone's clock indicates that it's evening or night. Although these hardware components seem fairly straightforward, the internal technology and software isn't that simple. It requires clever programming to make all of the elements work together for a fun, glitch-free game.

The initial release of Google Glass did not go as predicted; however, Google relaunched the technology in hopes of finding more success.

Many of the AR games available run similarly to *Pokémon Go*. The storylines and characters are all different. Users might be chasing zombies instead of Pokémon, for example. However, the basic technology is similar. The GPS, camera, compass, accelerometer, and clock help drive the gameplay.

However, not all AR is available solely with a smartphone. There are AR devices on the market, too, such as the Google Glass, which launched in 2013. Google Glass is a pair of eyeglasses that includes a camera and touchpad for interaction. Because AR involves overlaying objects onto a real-world view, Google Glass is ideal for the technology. Users see the real world through the glasses, but the technology can overlay software-generated objects over the real-world view.

Google Glass received mixed reviews when the technology was released. Production halted for a time. However, Google has resurrected the technology and has high hopes that its technological upgrades will make it a bigger player in the AR market. Although it has not been used widely in the gaming sector yet, it has found many practical uses for people working in engineering and manufacturing.

INNOVATION DRIVES JOBS

Although Google Glass did not necessarily meet Google's initial goals, developers continued to press forward. In fact, developers at Google created a new technology called Google Lens. It allows smartphone cameras to interact with the phone's software to search the internet using images. For instance, through this technology, a person could take a picture of a flower and learn what type of flower it is. This sort of innovation is what keeps the tech field moving forward. With its forward motion, there will continue to be a need for new people to fill new jobs.

3 VR AND AR JOBS IN GAMING

There are countless job opportunities available in the fields of VR and AR for gaming. Naturally, there are software engineers and programmers responsible for the computer programming needed for VR and AR games. Additionally, there are hardware engineers who create the headsets and controllers associated with VR. However, there are also content creators, user interaction and user experience engineers, 3D graphics artists, quality assurance (QA) engineers, and more. Given that the AR and VR global market was projected to reach more than $94 billion by 2023 by a 2018 market research report, it's an excellent time for

Opposite: The rise in use of AR and VR has made job opportunities in the field plentiful.

gaming enthusiasts to consider pursuing a career in AR or VR for gaming. Because the technology development path is similar for both AR and VR, all positions discussed in this chapter are relevant to both AR and VR careers in gaming.

SOFTWARE ENGINEER

Level:	Varies
Years of Experience Required:	Varies
Education Needed:	Bachelor's degree in computer science or a related field
Skills Needed:	Strong analytical and communication skills; creativity; attention to detail; strong problem-solving skills

There are a wide range of software engineering jobs in the VR and AR fields. Some don't necessarily require previous experience. However, some of the higher-level software engineering positions will require applicants to have experience.

For example, an entry-level VR software engineering position with tech giant Google requires applicants to have software development experience in at least one programming language. However, the company prefers that applicants also have experience using game engines, which are used to build video games. This experience, however, is not restricted to previous jobs. It could come from internships or from building games in your free time.

Depending on the software engineering job, the education needed also varies. That same Google position requires only a bachelor's degree in computer science or a related field (or equivalent practical experience in the field). However, the company prefers applicants to have a master's degree or a PhD in computer science, with an emphasis on graphics. Software engineer jobs in the AR/VR department of Apple have similar minimum and preferred requirements, as do jobs at Oculus.

However, for aspiring software engineers willing to take a chance on a smaller company or a start-up, there are positions available with lower minimum requirements. For example, one small San Francisco VR/AR developer advertised for candidates who have strong skills in specific programming languages with knowledge of computer graphics and familiarity with mathematics concepts. The company's job posting specifically stated that candidates did not need to be experts in VR and AR. The company was willing to teach those skills.

In general, though, a computer science degree will only help aspiring software engineers get their foot in the door at a VR/AR company. Additionally, programming experience (even if just in general gaming or a related area) will further increase marketability.

CONTENT CREATOR

Level:	Varies
Years of Experience Required:	Varies
Education Needed:	Varies
Skills Needed:	Strong creative vision and knowledge of story elements and narrative arc; ability to work productively with different teams; good communication skills

A VR or AR game can have amazing graphics and be remarkably immersive, but it won't attract dedicated gamers unless there's good content behind it. There needs to be a strong story, or gamers won't stay engaged. Someone needs to create the story behind a VR or AR game. That someone is a content creator—or, more likely, a team of content creators. These individuals are also sometimes called game designers.

Game development companies, whether for AR and VR or just for general video games, define the role of content creator in many ways. Some companies simply want the content creator to drive the artistic development of the game. In other words, companies want this person to

Content creators or game designers create the story of the game and the world in which the story takes place.

create the story, the ideas for graphics and environments, and so on. Other companies want the content creator to be skilled in programming and visual effects. This requires the person to have some sort of experience with computer science or programming. Due to these differing expectations of content creators, the job requirements for these positions vary widely.

For example, a content creator position for a VR company located in Detroit expected the VR content creator to work with the creative team to design and create the experience using Unreal or Unity. These are two major game engines that are used for development of video games and AR/VR content. The company also wanted applicants to be competent coders in Python, C#, and C, three common programming languages.

However, well-known game developer Electronic Arts expects their senior game designers to work with the design and production teams purely on content. This means that these individuals focus exclusively on how, for instance, characters and their skills impact the gamer's experience. For this position, there is no particular education needed. However, applicants at this senior level are expected to have at least five years of game-design experience and to have managed at least one gaming content project.

GRAPHIC ARTIST

Level:	Varies
Years of Experience Required:	Varies
Education Needed:	Bachelor's degree in 3D graphics, art and design, animation, computer science, or a related field
Skills Needed:	Experience with 3D graphics programs; at least a basic knowledge of game engines; knowledge of anatomy and animation; ability to effectively collaborate with others

Like many other jobs in AR and VR, graphic artist positions vary in their levels and requirements. Above all, however, 3D graphic artists need to have an artistic flair and a strong understanding of the software programs used to create and animate characters, objects, and environments in the game world.

In general, employers of graphic artists specializing in AR and VR expect applicants to have some higher education. Although companies usually expect applicants

VR AND AR IN THE CLASSROOM

perience the Sydney Opera House in 360°

Australian students use Google Cardboard to get a 360 degree view of the Sydney Opera House, further enhancing their field trip experience.

VR and AR are a lot of fun for games and experiences, but they can also be fantastic educational tools. For example, starting in 2015, schoolchildren got to take a virtual trip around the world when Google launched their Expeditions program. It works with the Google Cardboard, an inexpensive cardboard VR viewer.

Teachers have long taught about the geography and landscapes of faraway places, but they can bring the content up close and personal for students by taking them on virtual field trips using Expeditions. The students could climb mountains, scuba dive to explore the Great Barrier Reef, and much more. The Oculus Rift and other VR headsets can be used similarly. However, with limited school budgets, the Cardboard viewer is a much more affordable tool.

There are VR experiences that allow children to go back in time, too. They can experience the dinosaurs during the Jurassic age and battle during any of a number of wars. They can also learn about anatomy through VR. Developers have even created VR apps that let users experience what it may be like to live with autism, which can help students understand more about how some of their peers experience the world. While AR and VR are not widely used in schools yet, the possibilities for educational experiences are endless.

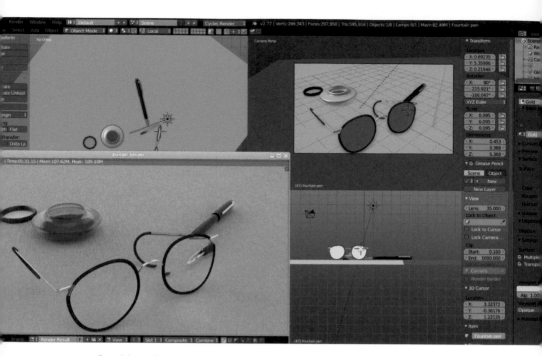

Graphic artists uses applications like Blender or Maya to create 3D art for AR and VR games and experiences.

to have at least a bachelor's degree, there are many degree programs applicable to this career. Some 3D graphic artists have a general degree in art and design, whereas others have more specialized degrees in 3D graphics. Others have general computer science degrees but strong artistic skills.

Experience requirements vary too. One company hiring a 3D artist for VR and AR prototypes required applicants to have a bachelor's degree and at least three years of experience as a professional 3D artist. In addition, the company wanted applicants to have at least a basic knowledge of game engines such as Unity and Unreal.

The company also required expert knowledge in texturing, lighting, rendering, and color. These skills are important as companies are interested in artists being able to create lifelike images through proper texturing and shading. Similarly, many of these companies want their graphic artists to have a basic knowledge of anatomy, rigging, and animation. Rigging is the creation of 3D model skeletons of animated figures before they are fully animated. A knowledge of anatomy is important so that graphic artists can rig a model that moves in lifelike fashion when it is fully animated.

As with the aforementioned jobs, some companies look for experience with specific software. For instance, some may want applicants who are trained in Blender, Maya, or another similar 3D modeling and animation software. However, familiarity with one of these programs helps individuals learn new ones.

Although VR and AR companies interested in hiring graphic artists don't always require previous AR or VR experience, they often express that applicants should be passionate and well-versed in the latest trends and tools in AR and VR. For gamers with an interest in AR/VR and an artistic flair, this is an ideal job that will likely continue to exist.

Think about a game, whether it's a regular video game or an AR/VR one. Today's games are incredibly detailed. AR/VR games and experiences are even more detailed in an attempt to make them as realistic and immersive as possible. This work would not be possible without graphic artists. Every AR/VR company in the world will require graphic artists to help them create ever more beautiful and realistic worlds, so the outlook for this particular job path is strong.

HARDWARE ENGINEER

Level:	Mid-level
Years of Experience Required:	Seven to ten years, depending on level of education
Education Needed:	Bachelor's or master's degree in electrical engineering or a related field
Skills Needed:	Experience with electrical engineering; experience working with software developers; proven record of advanced technology product development; strong collaborative skills

There are many hardware engineer jobs available in VR and AR. Headsets are constantly being developed and improved, as are hand controllers and sensors. There is even VR development in exoskeletons, or bodysuits that allow for a more immersive and responsive VR experience. These suits respond to virtual environments to provide users with a full-body experience. In general, though, hardware engineer positions in AR and VR are highly skilled, relatively advanced positions. They aren't necessarily management-level positions, but they aren't entry-level either.

For example, Oculus has a division called Core Tech that develops, designs, and tests cutting-edge VR technology. A hardware engineer position on the Core Tech team requires at least a bachelor's degree in electrical engineering. However, Oculus prefers applicants have a master's degree or PhD. Even with these degrees, experience is incredibly important. A recent graduate with a master's in electrical engineering isn't likely to walk out of the university and right into a hardware engineer job on the Core Tech team. They'll have to put in some years at a lower-level hardware engineering position to build up their experience.

Core Tech team members are expected to have at least seven years of experience in consumer product design. Additionally, Core Tech looks for at least seven years of experience in system-level design, including circuit design and debugging. Circuit design is related to the electrical wiring of the hardware. Debugging is related to solving system problems or defects.

The Core Tech team recruits hardware engineers who are strong collaborators and are able to manage projects that require input from multiple teams. In general, the ability to collaborate is important to most AR and VR employers. Employees must be able to work well with others. It's not enough to be a genius at electrical engineering.

Hardware engineers build the actual hardware that allows users to have VR and AR experiences.

QUALITY ASSURANCE (QA) ENGINEER

Level:	Entry-level
Years of Experience Required:	Varies
Education Needed:	Bachelor's degree in computer science or a related field
Skills Needed:	Strong deductive reasoning and analytical skills; attention to detail; ability to work independently; experience with bug-tracking software and testing tools; knowledge of common programming languages

Although coders and software developers are expected to troubleshoot and debug software as it's in development, they are human. Errors creep in. That's why tech companies have QA engineers. These specialists basically develop tests for new software and attempt to break it or cause issues. When they do break it, they work with development teams on how to resolve the problems. Only when the software is effectively break-proof is it released in beta form. This beta release is the first time that the software is available outside of the company. The software is usually offered to people trying out the product who might be interested in purchasing it in the future. During this beta release, the company that produced the software can collect feedback from users to further improve it.

As in any career, there are certainly advanced QA positions that are not entry-level. However, there are also many entry-level positions available at tech companies and in gaming and AR/VR. There are some QA jobs that require only an associate's degree, but most require at least a bachelor's degree in computer science or a related field.

Similarly, most companies hiring for a QA position prefer applicants to have some experience in QA or a related job. Oculus, for example, lists previous experience in its minimum qualifications but doesn't always specify how much previous experience is required. For aspiring QA engineers, any sort of related experience can only help with getting a foot in the door.

OTHER TYPES OF JOBS

Even if you're aren't particularly tech-savvy, you can still find roles in the VR and AR fields. In addition to the aforementioned roles, there are other jobs that involve marketing these VR/AR experiences at tech conferences or jobs that involve better understanding users' experiences. Perhaps you're really interested in research and VR technology but do not want to get a degree in computer science. A role as a user experience researcher might be just right for you. User experience researchers interview gamers about their experiences and gather market data to report back to the game companies about how people are enjoying the company's offerings. There are plenty of ways to get involved in this new and exciting field.

4 PLANNING FOR THE FUTURE

For students interested in a career in VR or AR for gaming, it's never too early to start preparing. There are classes and resources available to aspiring game developers. For instance, coding can be taken up as a hobby. There's nothing to stop interested students from learning to code in the comfort of their own home on their own computer.

DEGREE PROGRAMS FOR ASPIRING GAME DEVELOPERS

VR and AR are fairly new fields in the gaming world, so there aren't many degree programs specifically for VR and AR development. However, Ringling College

Opposite: Talent and technological skill can open doors to a career in the artistic side of AR and VR.

College isn't an absolute necessity for a career in AR or VR, but it will open many doors.

of Art and Design offers a VR development program. In it, students learn to design, create, and analyze VR in a variety of industries, one of which is gaming. The program's faculty are animators and designers in a variety of fields. They lead students through classes in everything from figure drawing to visual scripting, a visual programming language, to 2D and 3D design. The college also helps students find employment opportunities after graduation. However, this specialized and innovative program comes with a hefty price tag. In 2019, the annual cost for a student living on campus was about $67,000, with roughly $42,000 of that being tuition. Ringling does offer scholarships, grants, loans, and work-study programs, so financial aid is an option.

Ringling is far from the only program, though. VR-specific degrees are not the only option for those interested in a career in VR or AR in gaming. For most VR and AR gaming-related careers, a computer science degree is a good starting point. This type of degree program is offered at many colleges and universities. Some universities, such as Massachusetts Institute of Technology (MIT), Carnegie Mellon, and Stanford, are well known as top schools for computer science. However, many other state and private universities have good programs as well.

Additionally, in the gaming world, knowledge and experience are incredibly important. They can be more

Many degree programs in the field emphasize collaboration with peers on projects—just as in real-world careers in AR and VR.

important than where someone obtained his or her degree. An aspiring software engineer with a degree from a state university and a lot of experience in the field is every bit as likely to be considered for a position as a graduate from MIT who doesn't necessarily have much real-world experience. Since experience counts for a lot in the gaming world, students interested in a career in VR or AR for gaming should start building their experience early.

POTENTIAL COURSEWORK

In high school or middle school, students interested in a career in VR or AR for gaming can start to take classes that will help prepare them for the field. If classes in VR or AR are available, all the better! However, since these fields are fairly new, classes may not be available everywhere. Students can get started with computer science and digital art classes to form a solid foundation for their future career. Any courses in computer science are useful, such as classes on computer science theory; algorithms, or the sets of rules computers follow to problem-solve; and programming in practical languages such as C or C#.

Additionally, many community colleges allow high school students to take classes, either in person or online. In some cases, high school students can actually earn credits either at the high school level or toward their future college education for taking community college classes.

For a career in gaming, art classes are also useful. Most jobs in VR and AR for gaming involve some level of working with game art. For that reason, taking appropriate art classes early on will give students a leg up on the competition. Usually, classes that specialize in digital or graphic art and 3D modeling are excellent choices. Having a natural artistic flair is great, but not everyone has that. Students interested in a career in VR or AR for gaming shouldn't be discouraged if they aren't the next Picasso. Classes in digital art and 3D modeling can help even the least artistic among us gain the skills needed to be competitive in the field.

EXTRACURRICULAR ACTIVITIES

Most postings for AR and VR jobs in gaming share one common requirement. Applicants must be team-oriented. People in AR and VR must be good at collaboration because almost no piece of software or hardware is created by a single solitary developer or engineer. They are virtually all team efforts. Of course, there are the exceptional cases where someone develops a game completely on their own, working in the privacy of their own home. Some consider Palmer Luckey, the initial creator of the Oculus Rift, one such exception. However, it's important to know that Luckey simply created the prototype for the Rift. Before it went out to the mass market, it went through a development team at Oculus. Such is the case with most successful games or devices created by one person. They eventually go through teams of people to test their usability before being released to the mass market.

MAKING THE MOST OF SUMMER

Summer can be a time of relaxing, travel, or days spent by the pool. But it can also be a great time to gain some experience in a field of interest. A number of summer camps offer programs in VR and AR, including Emagination Tech Camps, Digital Media Academy's two-week VR Game Design camp for teens, Vision Tech Camp, iD Tech Camps, and Camp Galileo's VR camp. However, these camps can be expensive. Some, like Vision Tech and iD Tech Camps, offer scholarships to campers who cannot afford the full tuition. There are also more cost-effective options available. For example, the Boys & Girls Clubs in some areas offer tech camps, and their fees are much lower.

A new organization called TryEngineering.org also offers need-based scholarships to its Summer Institute for students across the United States. The program runs out of three university campuses: University of California Riverside, Texas A&M University, and Vaughn College of Aeronautics and Technology. While the camps aren't specifically about AR, VR, or even gaming, they focus on engineering challenges that help build skills applicable to those fields.

For high school students, internships may be an option too. In 2018, technology company Dell offered an internship program with their product engineering team near Austin, Texas. Internships for high schoolers are often unpaid. However, this particular program was a paid one in which the team of interns worked to create a virtual world that could generate real-world stimuli. The interns worked in teams to build various pieces of the VR world. The final product was a virtual room that had a fan in it. When the user turned on the fan in the VR room, it sent a signal to a real fan to blow air on the user.

Those interested in finding paid or unpaid internships should search the internet and the websites of various tech companies to see what's available. The right program could be right at your fingertips!

Online courses are a great way to learn about coding. Many colleges offer online courses that can be completed in the comfort of one's own home.

For that reason, it's important to demonstrate to employers your ability to work as part of a team. Middle school and high school students can demonstrate this ability by joining extracurricular clubs or sports teams. Playing lacrosse for four years may not seem like it has any particular relevance to AR and VR, but indirectly it does. It shows future employers that you can work as part of a team and have the dedication to stick with something important to you.

ADDITIONAL RESOURCES

Taking classes related to game development, art, and VR/AR is great, but not all knowledge has to be gained in a classroom setting. The great thing about coding, software development, and programming languages is that they can be learned anywhere, anytime, as there are online courses. Interested students can also simply get a book or look on the internet for information and resources.

Bookstores and libraries are full of "teach yourself" books about various programming languages and specifically about game development. For those who learn well from books, this is a great way to get started. Once an aspiring coder has the basics of a language down, the internet is full of further resources to develop more advanced skills in that language.

For those who prefer to learn online, there are some excellent web-based resources for learning. For example, Codecademy offers online coding tutorials for free. They offer courses in HTML, CSS, Java, JavaScript, and Python, among others—all of which are useful languages for aspiring game developers. For instance, HTML is an acronym for hypertext markup language. It is a computer language that uses standard words to define elements within a document. People use this computer language to create web pages and applications.

Most of Codecademy's online courses take fewer than eleven hours to complete. They feature coding quizzes and feedback from coaches and advisors, who are on hand to answer questions. Some programs are only offered with a Pro membership, which you have to pay for. However, there are many free courses to try as well.

The Unity 3D game engine and the Unreal engine are two of the most used game engines in game development. Both are free to use. In fact, Unity Technologies offers

This virtual space was created using 3ds Max. Students can subscribe to this software for up to three years for free. This gives them a substantial amount of time to learn the program.

many resources on its site to help users learn to work with Unity 3D and develop for it. They offer free tutorials and online projects. Additionally, the company provides live virtual training, free downloadable game kits, online support forums, and a user manual to help users get up to speed with the game engine. For a fee, you can also access online courses by Unity Certified Instructors.

Unreal Engine also offers many free resources. The Unreal Engine website offers example scenes and games created with Unreal, tutorials, and online support for those learning to develop with the engine.

There are also some great 3D art programs available online. However, some come at a cost. 3ds Max, for example, is a subscription-based 3D modeling and rendering program. It is a graphics package, which is an application used to create and manipulate images. Although it is a subscription-based program, there are free trials available. In fact, students can use it for free for three years. Autodesk, which makes 3ds Max, also offers Maya. It is a 3D animation, modeling, simulation, and rendering program. Like 3ds Max, Maya is subscription-based. However, students can also use Maya for three years for free. For both software applications, Autodesk offers online documentation, tutorials, downloads, videos, and more resources on its site.

Alternatively, there are free graphics packages, such as Blender. Aspiring developers can learn to work with a full-featured modeling, rendering, animation, and visual effects package for free. Future employers may want employees to know a specific graphics package, such as 3ds Max. However, a background in something like Blender is easily transferrable. Once a 3D artist or developer knows the ins and outs of one graphics package, it's not that hard to learn another one. Many job postings for AR and VR jobs will specifically ask for experience in a particular technology but then add "or related application" because they know that new software applications are fairly easily learned by someone with similar experience.

Hands-on learning is a fantastic way to learn some of the foundational skills that can help pave the way to a future career in VR and AR for gaming, so those with an interest in the field should jump in and get started.

5 EMERGING JOBS

The fields of VR and AR are fairly new in the grand scheme of the tech world. They are, however, growing rapidly. This rapid growth suggests that the fields will continue to grow in the coming years.

PROJECTED GROWTH IN VR AND AR

According to a 2017 market research report done by Orbis Research, the VR market was projected to surpass $40 billion by the year 2020. Please note that this figure represents the entire VR market, not just VR for gaming. The VR hardware market is growing particularly fast and is projected to continue growing, as is the software portion of the market. According to

Opposite: The demand for skilled professionals in VR and AR isn't likely to slow anytime soon.

the report, video game applications have accounted for the largest portion of the VR software market in recent years.

A 2017 market research report done by Zion Market Research predicted that the global AR market would reach more than $133 billion by 2021. This estimate anticipated a growth rate of more than 85 percent between 2016 and 2021. As with the forecast for VR, this was a prediction for the entire AR market, not just gaming.

It is important to remember that predictions about the market are just that: predictions. For instance, Orbis Research published a 2017 report indicating that the AR gaming market was likely to reach $284 billion by 2023. Obviously, the Zion and Orbis predictions differ significantly and cover slightly different time periods, which may account for some of the difference. Regardless, it's clear that market research companies and industry insiders expect the AR and VR gaming markets to grow extremely fast in the coming years as demand grows. Market growth means job growth, which means more opportunities for those interested in the field.

JOB MARKETS IN VR AND AR

Another important piece of information in the Orbis market report was the fact that several major tech companies accounted for more than 50 percent of those invested in the VR field in 2016. Those companies included Sony, Facebook, Google, and Samsung. For instance, Facebook owns Oculus—a giant in the VR industry. As of 2016,

Positions at large companies like Google can offer many attractive benefits, in addition to competitive salaries.

Microsoft ranked relatively low in the VR market. However, that number is expected to change as Microsoft invests more in VR and AR development.

Positions at Large Companies

For those interested in a career in VR and AR for gaming, finding a job at a company like Oculus would be ideal. Oculus is on the cutting edge of VR. The company boasts competitive salaries, full health-care coverage, a strong retirement program, free meals, flexible work schedules, generous vacation policies, and access to the latest Oculus prototypes and products. Typically, Oculus hires for software engineers, hardware engineers, research scientists and engineers, artists and product designers, and quality

Although there are other uses of AR and VR, such as in the field of engineering, these technologies have remained incredibly popular in gaming. In fact, other industries, like the military, rely on the innovative work of game developers who work at both large companies and start-ups.

assurance engineers. They also typically have internships available for college and graduate students.

Most of the major tech companies offer similar employment packages and perks. In fact, major tech companies are known for having some fun perks. The perks vary by company and location. However, some tech employees report fun perks like having access to free on-site gyms and getting to bring their pets to work.

Positions at Start-Ups

Not everyone will land a job at a major tech company. However, there are plenty of tech start-ups working in VR and AR too. Working at start-ups can be risky as not every start-up is successful. When start-ups are

Start-up jobs can be exciting for those wanting to work with a company from the ground up. They do, however, come with some risks. There can be less job security in these companies.

unsuccessful, people lose their jobs. That said, there is a lot of excitement and possibility that comes with working for a start-up company. For example, development teams at start-up tech companies are usually much smaller. This small team size allows each member to take on more responsibility. It also allows them to gain more experience in different areas. Instead of specializing in one very specific area of VR or AR development, members of a start-up team may get to work on several different parts of the project.

Similarly, the chance to create is often greater in a start-up. At a major company, employees are cogs in a much larger machine, as the saying goes. They are all important, and they all work together toward a common goal. However, their own role can be very small and narrowly defined. At a tech start-up, the culture often encourages innovation. Start-up owners are themselves innovators. Employees get the benefit of learning from them and are often encouraged in their own innovation.

The chances to move up in the company can also be more plentiful. If the start-up grows quickly, employees who were there from day one can quickly advance through the ranks to a more senior position. These higher positions usually come with more benefits and higher pay. If the start-up becomes extremely successful, the financial rewards can be great. Start-up companies often offer fairly low salaries because they simply don't have the budget for high salaries. To compensate their employees for the lower-than-average pay, they sometimes offer stock options that can prove to be very valuable if the company ends up succeeding in a big way. Imagine the salaries for the first employees at Microsoft, when it was a tiny start-up. Then look at the net worth of some of its initial employees who got in on the ground floor. Many of those early employees have become very, very rich.

Finally, there is also a certain pride of ownership that can come in working for a start-up. People who are part of a small team that creates something amazing generally feel pride in what their small team accomplished. It's an environment where contributors can really see their work in action.

Whatever employment and educational path VR and AR enthusiasts choose in the coming years, it's likely there will be plenty of jobs in this exciting and cutting-edge industry!

ON THE CUTTING EDGE

VR and AR technologies are themselves on the cutting edge, but there are facets of these technologies that are even more astounding than others. For example, VR can create stunningly realistic and immersive virtual worlds for games. Additionally, facial-recognition technology can allow gamers to create remarkably realistic custom avatars for their characters. An avatar is a visual representation of a player in a video game.

Intel's RealSense technology can read emotions and create strikingly realistic avatars.

Now, Intel has created a RealSense 3D camera that could theoretically allow VR games to adapt based on the emotions reflected in a player's face. The camera scans seventy-eight points on a person's face to read the person's emotions. The game world could then adapt to the player's emotions. If the camera reads fear in the player's face, the game might lessen its intensity, for example.

The RealSense cameras can also take 3D information from a player's environment, as well as judge depth. This technology helps create images that are more useful for positioning during VR game play, which improves the gamer's immersive experience.

Considering the fact that simple digital cameras didn't become commonplace until the mid- to late 1990s, it's pretty amazing to think of a camera that can contribute significantly to virtual reality and interaction with the virtual world.

GLOSSARY

accelerometer An instrument or application that measures the speed and direction of movement.

algorithm A set of rules computers follow in order to problem-solve.

augmented reality (AR) This type of computer programming adds computer-generated elements to a user's existing field of vision through devices like smartphones or smart glasses.

avatar A visual representation of a person in a video game or on the internet.

beta Software that is in a testing phase.

exoskeleton A wearable bodysuit that can allow VR users to more fully interact with the virtual world by creating physical sensations in response to virtual events.

game engine A software development environment that software engineers can use to build video games.

global positioning system (GPS) This technology uses satellites to pinpoint a device's location.

graphics package An application used to create and manipulate images.

hardware The physical equipment that allows for AR and VR experiences, like headsets and controllers.

HTML An acronym for hypertext markup language, a programming language used to create web pages and applications.

patent A legal document that gives an individual or a company the legal right to be the sole creator of an invention for a given amount of time.

programming language A series of commands and instructions used to make a computer perform certain tasks or to create a software program.

prototype The initial model of a product that can be tested and recreated.

rendering This is the process through which images are generated from a 2D or 3D model by means of computer programs.

rigging The process of creating a digital skeleton for an animated character so that it can be programmed to move.

software Programmed instructions that are stored and run inside of hardware to make VR and AR equipment work.

virtual reality (VR) This type of computer programming uses graphics, sounds, and other sensory stimuli to make users feel as if they are inside of a digital environment.

wireframe A skeletal 3D model in which only lines and vertexes, or points, are shown.

FURTHER INFORMATION

Books

Henneberg, Susan. *Virtual Reality*. Opposing Viewpoints. Farmington Hills, MI: Greenhaven Press, 2017.

Hulick, Kathryn. *Virtual Reality Developer*. San Diego: ReferencePoint Press, 2017.

Moritz, Jeremy. *Code for Teens: The Awesome Beginner's Guide to Programming*. Herndon, VA: Mascot Books, 2018.

Strom, Chris. *3D Game Programming for Kids: Create Interactive Worlds with JavaScript*. Raleigh, NC: Pragmatic Bookshelf, 2018.

Vaidyanathan, Sheena. *Creative Coding in Python: 30+ Programming Projects in Art, Games, and More*. Beverly, MA: Quarry Books, 2018.

Websites

Bureau of Labor Statistics: Occupational Outlook Handbook

https://www.bls.gov/ooh/computer-and-information -technology/home.htm

This website provides career data concerning responsibilities, education and training required, pay, and outlook for computer and information technology jobs.

Lynda

https://www.lynda.com

Lynda is an online learning service that is now part of LinkedIn Learning. It is a fee-based service that offers more than six hundred courses in software development, more than seven hundred courses in design, and more than seven hundred courses in web development. Interested aspiring developers can sign up for a free month to try out courses.

Microsoft Virtual Academy

https://mva.microsoft.com

This site offers free online training courses for developers and people interested in information technology.

Videos

Building Augmented Reality Experiences with Unity3D - Abhishek Singh - CS50 Tech Talk

https://www.youtube.com/watch?v=_xJBScA9mpw

New York University graduate Abhishek Singh discusses different types of augmented reality, the hardware associated with AR, and how to develop AR experiences.

How Augmented Reality Will Change Education Completely

https://www.youtube.com/watch?v=5AjxGqzqQ54

This video is a TEDx talk by brand marketing and communications expert Florian Radke about how augmented reality can move beyond being a toy to being a useful educational tool.

SELECTED BIBLIOGRAPHY

"Augmented Reality (AR) Market (Sensor, Display, and Software) for Aerospace & Defense, Industrial, Consumer, Commercial, E-commerce, Retail and Other Applications: Global Industry Perspective, Comprehensive Analysis, Size, Share, Growth, Segment, Trends, and Forecast, 2015–2021." Zion Market Research, November 23, 2016. https://www.zionmarketresearch.com/report/augmented-reality-market.

"Developer Satisfaction Survey 2016." International Game Developers Association, November 4, 2016. https://cdn.ymaws.com/www.igda.org/resource/resmgr/files__2016_dss/IGDA_DSS_2016_Summary_Report.pdf.

Fagan, Kaylee. "Here's What Happens to Your Body When You've Been in Virtual Reality for Too Long." *Business Insider*, March 4, 2018. https://www.businessinsider.com/virtual-reality-vr-side-effects-2018-3.

"Global Augmented Reality (AR) and Virtual Reality (VR) Market Is Forecast to Reach $94.4 Billion by 2023 – Soaring Demand for AR & VR in the Retail & E-commerce Sectors." *PR Newswire*, July 31,

2018. https://www.prnewswire.com/news-releases/
global-augmented-reality-ar-and-virtual-reality-vr-
market-is-forecast-to-reach-94-4-billion-by-2023---
soaring-demand-for-ar--vr-in-the-retail--e-commerce-
sectors-300689154.html.

"Global Virtual Reality Market (Hardware and
Software) and Forecast to 2020." Orbis Research,
February 6, 2017. http://www.orbisresearch.com/
reports/index/global-virtual-reality-market-
hardware-and-software-and-forecast-to-2020.

Greenwald, Will. "Oculus Rift vs. HTC Vive: Which
Virtual Reality Headset Is Best?" *PC Magazine*, June
22, 2018. https://www.pcmag.com/compare/361805/
oculus-rift-vs-htc-vive.

McKie, Robin. "Virtual Reality Headsets Could
Put Children's Health at Risk." *Guardian*,
October 28, 2017. https://www.theguardian.com/
technology/2017/oct/28/virtual-reality-headset-
children-cognitive-problems.

Orbis Research. "Augmented Reality (AR) Gaming Market 2017–2023: Industry Analysis by Drivers, Restraints, Opportunities, Trends, and Forecasts to 2023." Reuters, July 13, 2017. https://www.reuters.com/brandfeatures/venture-capital/article?id=12766.

P&S Market Research. "Augmented Reality and Virtual Reality Market by Devices, by Component, by Application, by Geography – Global Market Size, Share, Development, Growth, and Demand Forecast, 2013–2023." Research and Markets, June 2018. https://www.researchandmarkets.com/research/6w5hhb/global_augmented?w=5.

Simonite, Tom. "Google Glass Is Back—Now with Artificial Intelligence." Wired, July 25, 2018. https://www.wired.com/story/google-glass-is-backnow-with-artificial-intelligence.

Tokareva, Julia. "The Difference Between Virtual Reality, Augmented Reality and Mixed Reality." Forbes, February 2, 2018. https://www.forbes.com/sites/quora/2018/02/02/the-difference-between-virtual-reality-augmented-reality-and-mixed-reality/#41407e322d07.

"Virtual Reality Development." Ringling College of
Art and Design. Accessed January 15, 2019. https://
www.ringling.edu/VirtualReality.

Wakefield, Jane. "The Real-World Uses for Virtual
Reality." BBC News, October 24, 2016. https://www.
bbc.com/news/technology-37576755.

Warner, Claire. "How Does 'Pokemon Go' Work? Here's
Everything We Know About the Tech Behind the
Augmented Reality Fad." *Bustle*, July 13, 2016.
https://www.bustle.com/articles/172317-how-does-
pokemon-go-work-heres-everything-we-know-about-
the-tech-behind-the-augmented-reality.

INDEX

Page numbers in **boldface** refer to images.

ABOUT THE AUTHOR

Cathleen Small is the author of more than sixty books for students in middle school and high school. Before making the switch to writing, Small was an editor for a technical publisher for nearly twenty years, where she edited hundreds of books on game development, programming, applications, and more. When she's not writing, Small enjoys traveling and spending time with her family in the San Francisco Bay Area.